THE WAR NEXT DOOR

Tamsin Oglesby

THE WAR NEXT DOOR

OBERON BOOKS
LONDON

First published in 2007 by Oberon Books Ltd
521 Caledonian Road, London N7 9RH
Tel: 020 7607 3637 / Fax: 020 7607 3629
e-mail: info@oberonbooks.com
www.oberonbooks.com

A catalogue record for this book is available from the British
Library.

ISBN: 1 84002 729 0 / 978-1-84002-729-7

Cover image: Graham Caws

Printed in Great Britain by Antony Rowe Ltd, Chippenham

Characters

ALI

MAX

SOPH

HANA

BOBBY

The War Next Door was first performed on 1 February 2007 at the Tricycle Theatre, with the following company:

ALI, Jonathan Coyne
MAX, David Michaels
SOPH, Lorraine Burroughs
HANA, Badria Timimi
BOBBY, Sonny Muslim

Director Nicolas Kent
Designer Libby Watson
Lighting Designer Lucy Carter
Sound Designer Adam Cork

Scene 1

Early evening. Sounds of the city: mumbling conversation; a fox barking; a car alarm; laughter; a plaintive song; a distant argument.

An explosion of music. The sound of shouting can be heard underneath.

BOBBY comes running out of the house with his hands over his ears. He fumbles in his pocket and produces an air pistol. Takes aim and fires off one bullet after another at a target. A bird flies over; as an afterthought he aims at it. To his horror, it falls to the ground. He bends over it, distraught.

Scene 2

ALI and MAX in MAX's house.

ALI   Man I have no problem with your wife,
       man, she's a nice lady and all
       but you got to tell her – on my life –
       I can see everything over that wall
       I'm that far from calling the cops
       she's running about stark naked out there
       (cept for a pair a flip flops)
       you got to go tell her
       (I can't, you're her fellah, you can)
       put some fuckin clothes on, man.

MAX   I'm sorry, I had no idea –

ALI   Get outta here
       she's in your garden now innit

go and have a look, see –
one minute she's lyin down
next she's jumpin about like a flea.

MAX   No. No, I know she's *there*
it just didn't occur to me that anyone would care.

ALI   Come off it mate –
what am I supposed to do?
How'm I supposed to concentrate,
that kinda view?
I'm jus tryin to eat my food
I turn my head that way
she's right outside my window in the fucking *nude*
what, you think I'm gay?

MAX   I can see, Ali, no, I can see you feel
it's an invasion of your space –

ALI   Thank you, yes, thank you
I'm talking right in my face
and she does these exercise
all day long –
you know your wife can do the splits?
(remember, nothing on)
I look out my window I don't want no surprise
I look out my window I want to see flowers, trees, grass
don't want to be looking up nobody's arse.

MAX   Look, I'm sorry, alright, but the thing is, Ali
I'm sure she didn't realise anyone could see.

ALI   You're joking me, man
you'd have to be blind
and it's not just me as reached my limit.

MAX   What do you mean?

ALI   She's gonna have a baby innit
          she got all that to think of now
          she got her pride
          she can't go walking around like a cow
          all that going on the other side.

MAX   A baby. But that's great.

ALI   Yeah, whatever.

MAX   No, Congratulations, Ali. That's amazing.

ALI   Easy mate, not clever.

MAX   When's it due?

ALI   Listen – I don't know – what I'm saying is
          we like you and all that shit
          but what you gonna do about it?

MAX   The thing is Ali, technically –

ALI   She wouldda come round herself –

MAX   Technically speaking –

ALI   She can't though, can she, she's on nights.

MAX   Soph is in her own garden, / so technically –

ALI   But she feels the same as me, innit.

MAX   She is within her garden, therefore within her rights.

ALI   You what?

MAX   It's a question of property.

ALI   No.

MAX   It's a question of property / and I think you'll find the

ALI   No, it's a question of, no, it's a question of privacy,

MAX   law says if she's on her own property –

ALI   *privacy*, innit. We overlook your wife – I mean your
        property – so
        that's the question. Legally –

MAX   Thing is Ali, listen mate, / thing is I think you'll find

ALI   No, legally though –

MAX   the other neighbours don't mind.

ALI   That's because they can't see.

MAX   Why not?

ALI   Because of the fucking tree.

MAX   Look, mate, I'm a reasonable bloke
        and I appreciate the visit
        and all that, but what exactly is it
        you want from me?
        You want to talk about the fucking oak?
        I told you this before – it's old, I can't just cut it down –
        it was planted in sixteen fifty-three.
        Or you want to complain about Soph?
        Alright. So. She's naked in the garden.
        I'm sorry if it's giving you a – a – *headache* –
        but what do you want me to say?
        This is the twenty-first century, Ali
        I'm not gonna tell her to put it away.

ALI   No, you're the boss. Simple. You decide.
        You cover her up, or she goes inside.

MAX   But she's just lying there –

ALI   She's not jus lyin there, that's what I said,
      she's got her legs up over her head
      / and she's jumpin about with her arse in the air –

MAX   Alright, okay, but listen, alright, Ali
      look at it this way
      you have to admit
      (I know I'm married to her so I would say)
      but at least she's fit.

ALI   You say?

MAX   Never mind.

ALI   So maybe she's cute
      she might be a minger all I care
      that's not the question I'm here to dispute.

MAX   Quite right.

ALI   No offence mate.

MAX   None taken.

ALI   Cos she in't.

MAX   What?

ALI   Ugly.

MAX   I know.

ALI   You're a lucky bloke
      alright, but that int the point.

MAX   I know. I shouldn't have said anything.
      You fancy a joint?

ALI   You what?

MAX   Smoke?

ALI   No.

MAX   Dope I'm talking dope.

ALI   No, cheers, mate, no.

MAX   This isn't your usual runothemill. I grow it myself in the
        garden.
        Come on, mate. I insist.
        You'll never find better grass anywhere.

ALI   I don't smoke.

MAX   Don't tell me. You'd rather get pissed.

ALI   No. I just prefer coke.

MAX   Right.

ALI   Smoking makes me go yellow.

MAX   Not this stuff, it doesn't, no,
        this just makes you mellow
        grown out the back with my own fair hand
        (purely recreational, you understand)
        I started with a patch out there by the wall
        – this is last year, now I've got a bloody jungle –
        I promise you, mate, it's top, this is
        have some now and take some for the missus.

ALI   Doesn't it make you lose your, you know, type thing.

MAX   Trust me, no,
        if anything it's good for your libido
        I'm not saying it's viagra,
        but if that's what you're after
        a couple of puffs should be enough for a decent shag or
        two.
        (Not with me, obviously)

ALI   And it don't make you vomit?

MAX   Only if you were to swallow it.

        Pause.

ALI   Go on then.

MAX   Good man. Here you go.
        The secret is take it slow.

        *MAX hands him a joint and smokes one himself. After a
        while:*

        What do you think? You like it?

ALI   Nice one.

MAX   See what I mean? It's top.

ALI   It's kind of

MAX   Isn't it?

ALI   Makes you feel

MAX   Calm?

ALI   No, makes you feel

MAX   Cool. Hot?

ALI   No.

MAX   What?

ALI   Makes you feel all –

MAX   horny.

ALI   No. What's the word? What's the word?

MAX   What? Happy? What? High? What?

ALI   Yeah, like a like a like a –

MAX   Bird?

ALI   Makes me feel tall.

MAX   That's nice.

ALI   And empty.

MAX   Empty. Tall and empty. Nice, yeah.
        Is that nice?

ALI   Like, yeah, like tall and cool and empty like, you know,
        like

MAX   A model.

ALI   No, like like a

MAX   Like a glass of ice?

ALI   No, more like a hole, you know, a hole.

MAX   Yeah. like, yeah, like, like a hole, yeah.
        What kind of hole?

ALI   I don't want to go into what kind of hole.

MAX   Is it a nice hole?

ALI   It's quiet.

MAX   A nice quiet hole. There you are then
        best marijuana money can buy.

ALI   How'd you spell it? / Marijuana –

MAX   I don't I don't. I told you, it's just for me and my mates.

ALI   What?

MAX   It's for my own pleasure. I'm not interested in cash.

ALI   What you talkin about?
Oh, man, this is wicked, this hash
look at your face.

ALI starts giggling.

MAX   What?

ALI   Look, just look at your face.

MAX   That's the second phase
where you find everything funny.

ALI   No man, whichever way you look at it
you crack me up.
This stuff is right on the money.

MAX   What's wrong with my face?

ALI continues laughing, then stops abruptly.

ALI   Oh, I feel oh, I feel like crying now.

MAX   Woh. Crying's the last phase. You skipped a few.

ALI   I'm not *gonna* cry.

MAX   You want to cry? Cry.

ALI   I'm not gonna cry. I just feel like it.

MAX   Why?

ALI   I dunno.

MAX   Doesn't matter if you want to cry.
You just got there quick is all I'm saying.

ALI   I want to cry about?
My woman's gonna have a fucking kid
why'd I want to start crying?

MAX   I don't know, we should be celebrating.

ALI   Tell me to cry.

MAX   I'm not saying – it doesn't matter if you did –
        whatever you're feeling – you don't have to explain
        it makes me want to do all sorts of things
        cartwheels on the ceiling
        handstands in the rain.

ALI   Go on then. Do a fucking handstand.

MAX   I can't do fucking handstands can I?

ALI   I dunno.

MAX   Well I can't.

ALI   Alright.

MAX   I can't alright, but it's not like I'm complaining.

ALI   Tha's cool.

MAX   Anyway it isn't raining.

        SOPH shouts from offstage.

SOPH   Quickly Max, quick, there's a fox in the garden!

MAX   Shit.

ALI   Fuck.

SOPH   There's a fox in the garden Max quick!

MAX   (*Pushing ALI's head down.*) Duck

ALI   I gotta get out.

MAX   No, no, no, no. Stay.

ALI   She coming in? I gotta get out. / I gotta get out.

MAX   No, don't worry, she won't come in this way.

SOPH   Where are you? Max? Where are you?

ALI   Why can't I go? Where is she?

MAX   Other side of the wall.

ALI   Let me out.

MAX   I can't.

ALI   You can.

MAX   I can't. You'd see her in the hall.

SOPH   MAX!

MAX   She's coming in.

ALI   No!

MAX   Alright, alright, it's okay, don't go.

ALI   Shut the door shut the door shut the door, man.

MAX   There isn't one. It's open plan.

       ALI turns round and covers his eyes.

       Hang on, Soph, I'm coming.

       SOPH walks in wearing a sarong.

SOPH   There's a fox out there, are you deaf?
       There's a fox in the middle of the lawn
       right in the middle of the day
       – I've been shouting –
       just standing there looking all forlorn
       but he won't go away.
       Alright, Ali? Come and see. It's alright
       he's beautiful. He won't bite.

ALI doesn't respond. He still has his hands over his eyes.

MAX   He thought you didn't have any clothes on.

SOPH   I didn't.

MAX   But you do now. She does now Ali. She's wearing a
       sarong.

SOPH   I was just lying there, with my eyes closed
        when I felt this wet nose
        nudging me.
        I shot right up
        he was looking at me nastily
        like the fox who couldn't get the grapes.
        He's probably only a cub –
        quick, come and see him before he escapes.

SOPH goes over to the window

MAX   It's alright Ali. Listen. She's got something on.

SOPH   Oh I don't believe it. He's gone.

MAX   Ali, you can turn round now.

SOPH   He must have jumped over the fence.

ALI takes his hands off his eyes and MAX turns him round.

MAX   See.

SOPH   Quick brown fox. He has, he's run away.

ALI makes to leave.

MAX   No stay Ali, relax, it's okay.

ALI   I gotta go.

SOPH   Well you would if you had any sense
        wouldn't you? It's unnatural, don't you think?

You don't hang around like that in broad daylight.
I've never seen them stand like that and stare.
They say foxes stink
but I didn't smell a thing and he was standing right
  there.
Do they have foxes in in in in –

ALI   No.

MAX   More likely wolves.

SOPH   Oh my god. A wolf in your back garden, can you
       imagine?

MAX   I don't think they have back gardens either.

SOPH   Alright, no. How's Hana?

MAX   She's pregnant.

SOPH   Oh my god.

MAX   Isn't that great?

SOPH   Is that why –
       yes, congratulations, Ali, that's great.
       Is that why we haven't seen much of her lately?

ALI   She just don't like going out.

SOPH   Oh but she must. She must come round and celebrate.
       She wouldn't like to clean for us, would she?

ALI   Clean?

SOPH   Only we've just lost ours. Said the house was too dirty.
       Snotty little Polak. Spent the whole time flirting.
       If Hana was interested that would be nice.
       It wouldn't be too hard
       and she could just come through the back yard.

ALI   Too busy.

SOPH   Absolutely, no, that's fine.

ALI   She an't got time.

SOPH   Of course.
        She is a cleaner, isn't she?
        Only I wouldn't ask her, obviously.
        If she wasn't. A cleaner.

ALI   She's on nights.

SOPH   Of course of course of course she is.

ALI   I gotta go.

SOPH   That's why we haven't seen her.

MAX   No, look, Ali, stay, sit down.
        We were just having a smoke.

ALI   Gotta go now.

MAX   No, don't. We've hardly started.
        Sophie, go and put some clothes on.

SOPH   I beg your pardon.

MAX   Sorry.

SOPH   Don't talk to me like that.

        Unnoticed by the others, ALI slips out.

MAX   I'm sorry, it's just –

SOPH   What's wrong with my sarong?

MAX   You don't like me smoking.

SOPH   You want me to go ask me nicely.
        Don't make up specious reasons
        and treat me like some doormat.

MAX   Would you please go?

SOPH   No.

        MAX, looking round, notices ALI's gone.

MAX   He's gone.

SOPH   What did he want anyway?

MAX   A chat.
        He was upset because you were naked outside.
        Look, I'm sorry if I was blunt –

SOPH   He's upset because I was naked outside?
        Well I'm upset because of him being a cunt.
        You remember to tell him that?

MAX   Slipped my mind.

SOPH   You should tell him we *know*.

MAX   What?

SOPH   You should tell him.

MAX   We don't know.

SOPH   Of course we do.

MAX   We don't.

SOPH   The trouble with you is you're far too nice.
        Sorry I'm middle class, sorry I'm white, sorry I'm richer
          than you, you are – you sound so servile.

MAX   Just because I'm white and middle class
doesn't mean I like it up the arse.
I also have, as you well know, enormous reserves of
    bile.

SOPH   Don't be crass.
I'm just saying it's going to make it harder when the
    time comes.
A volte face. It will be. A complete volte face.

MAX   You go and see her. She's pregnant.
You'll have something to talk about.

SOPH   Oh god.

MAX   What?

SOPH   That's when they're at their most volatile, you know.
When the woman gets pregnant or threatens to go.
The thought just makes me sick.

MAX   Do you think she'll ever leave him?

SOPH   Who knows? He's such a prick.
I certainly bloody well hope so.

Scene 3

SOPH on HANA's doorstep

SOPH   Hello.

HANA   You can't come in.

SOPH   No, it's okay, that's alright
I just thought I'd give you a shout
and see if you'd got your new bin.
Only I noticed, I think, you hadn't put it out.

HANA   Is a mess.

SOPH   It's okay, I don't want to come in
        – it's green.

HANA   I know. They been. They come and been.

SOPH   We, for some reason, were given two
        so I've brought you the spare –
        here – it's for you.

HANA   No, s'alright.

SOPH   You know it's not such a chore
        you don't need to separate it out anymore
        bottles and tins and cardboard and plastic
        you just chuck it all in, it's fantastic.
        They do all the sorting at some local base
        much better than before
        when it all went overseas to dodgy developing countries
        like China
        because the biggest problem we face
        today (apart from the imminent self destruction of the
           entire human race)
        is how to find a use for all the rubbish we produce
        because of course the old days, no one had a car
        and you'd never buy more than you could carry or eat
        so you did all your shopping in the high street
        but now, my god, the stuff we discard!
        Did you know, every two hours
        we throw away enough to fill the Albert Hall
        – all things you could recycle –
        we've been on at the council for years, me and Max,
        proves it's worth making a fuss
        you know we use eight billion carrier bags annually?
        Britain, that is, not us.

        Pause.

HANA   We got three.

SOPH   Sorry?

HANA   Bins.

SOPH   That's good then. Right. Okay.
         Oh congratulations Hana! I nearly forgot to say.
         When's it due?

HANA   I int pregnant. Jus fat innit.

SOPH   No, Hana, you're not fat.

HANA   Well I int pregnant. What make you say that?

SOPH   Ali said.

HANA   He don't know his ass from his head.
         I'm no havin no baby. Still got the boy round the house.

SOPH   Oh yes, Bobby. But he's at school
         isn't he?

HANA   Yeah but he don't hardly go in
         just hangs about, thinks he's cool
         don't know what's wrong with him.

SOPH   It's funny, I've always thought but he looks nothing like
         you.

HANA   Tha's because he in't mine.

SOPH   Oh.

HANA   Ali's first wife.

SOPH   Right, yeah, fine.
         You're not having a baby then?

HANA   No. I wouldn't mind a girl but he only wants boys.
         You come round to complain about the noise?

SOPH   Hold on a minute.

HANA   It's the elephant innit.

SOPH   What elephant?

HANA   You must of heared?

SOPH   What?

HANA   This morning through the wall.

SOPH   I didn't hear nothing – anything – this morning, no.

HANA   Shouting his mouth off. I told him shuttup.

SOPH   No, nothing at all –
        maybe before we were up.

HANA   It's the elephant in the front room innit.

SOPH   The elephant.

HANA   Yeah.

SOPH   In the room?

HANA   I said he shouldn't even been there.
        You know the one what I mean.

SOPH   Well. I didn't want to presume.
        But since you mention it.

HANA   He jus gets in the way.
        But he went crazy when he seen
        what happ. I say to him I say
        it's you what bring him in
        but it's me as gets the blame for him.

SOPH   There's no excuse
        but that'll be his shame speaking.

HANA   He shouldn't even be in it.
        Big elephant.
        I shouldda jus bin it.
        You can't have thing like that inside
        you must of heared it when he fell.

SOPH   It's yes, I think, eventually,
        that's the thing – it's something you can't hide.

HANA   I didn't mean to knock him over,
        he make me beg
        him to forgivin me but it wan't my fault
        I was jus cleanin
        then I see I break his leg.

SOPH   You broke *his* leg?

HANA   Big mistake.
        He only found out this morning
        – is quite a big break –
        his foot was comin off the, you know, at the end.

SOPH   Jesus.

HANA   S'okay I says to him. He'll mend.

SOPH   Did you call an ambulance?

HANA   What?

SOPH   I know they're always late
        but they do come eventually
        you just have to wait
        – no really, whatever he's done, I really think you
          should.

HANA   You crazy? It's a elephant. Is made a wood.

SOPH   What're you talking about?

HANA   What you talkin about?

SOPH   The elephant in the room?

HANA   Tha's what I'm sayin. It shouldn't be there.

SOPH   The elephant.

HANA   Not in a room.

SOPH   You mean – oh I don't understand. You mean a *real*
        elephant?

HANA   No I mean wood elephant innit.
        You think because I'm foreign I'm a idiot?

SOPH   Oh I thought I thought – Jesus, no, I thought – oh I see.

        Pause.

HANA   So, what, you didn't hear nothing?

SOPH   When? No, not, no, not today.

HANA   Them walls must be thick.

SOPH   Yes, they must, mustn't they.

HANA   You never heard us?

SOPH   No. Not a thing. No
        I mean, sometimes – well –
        you ever hear us?

HANA   Oh yes.

SOPH   Oh.

HANA   Sometime I hear you shout, sometime I hear your
        husband cuss. Sometime I hear you sing.

SOPH   I'm sorry. You should have said.

HANA   Don't matter. You sing nice.

SOPH   Well thank you.

HANA   But I give you a piece advice.
         It goes like this. Amazing grace
         how sweet the *sound* that save a wretch like me. Not *face*.

Scene 4

SOPH and MAX. Loud music and the sound of muffled shouting coming from next door.

BOBBY runs into the garden with his air pistol. Sets up a target. Then decides not to bother with it. He looks into the air instead, and, spotting a bird, takes aim and fires. He misses. Tries again. And again.

SOPH   Oh god, not again.

MAX   And it's only Tuesday.

SOPH   What are they saying? What did he say?

MAX   Who knows.

SOPH   Can you see?

MAX   Curtain's closed.

SOPH   What do you think he's doing though?

MAX   You look if you want. Don't ask me.

SOPH   I don't want to see, but I need to *know*.

         MAX cranes to see out the window. SOPH behind him.

MAX   Oh god.

SOPH   What? Don't tell me don't tell me don't tell me. What's
        he doing?

MAX   I'm not telling you.

SOPH   Why not?

MAX   Because I can't see. All I can see is their shadow.

SOPH   What's it doing? (I can't stand this)

MAX   He looks like he's got something in his hand. / It looks

SOPH   What?

MAX   like – no – he's just waving his fist.

SOPH   Waving it? Just waving it? What do you mean?

MAX   No, he has, he's got something in it.

SOPH   Does it involve a weapon? We can't just sit here if it
        involves a weapon. That would be obscene.

MAX   You look.

SOPH   I'm not looking.

MAX   It's a cigarette.

SOPH   That's not a weapon. Is it lit?

MAX   Depends what you do with it.
        Yes.

SOPH   I mean like a knife. What is he doing with it? What's
        happening?

        HANA screams.

MAX   She's screaming.

SOPH   I can hear that.

ALI shouts.

MAX   He's shouting. It looks like they're dancing.

SOPH   People don't scream when they're dancing.

MAX   People do exactly scream when they're dancing.

SOPH   Not where I come from they don't.

MAX   Where does he come from again? / No, I've forgotten.

SOPH   I've told you so many times, you prat.
       He's Eastern – middle-eastern-european – Turkistan is
         it?
       I don't know, somewhere like that.

MAX   What about her?

SOPH   No, she's from somewhere else.

MAX   Oh yes, that's right.

SOPH   What's he doing now?

MAX   Looks like he's holding her. Tight.

SOPH   Phone the police. Or knock on the door.
       Say they're disturbing our peace.
       Or just ask for some sugar. Go on.

MAX   Why would I want sugar? I don't cook.

SOPH   They don't know that. And you don't need to cook to
         use sugar. Sugar you can put on your cereal.

MAX   It's ten o' clock at night.

SOPH   Oh for fuck's sake.

MAX   You go. You can say you're making a cake.

SOPH   Don't be stupid. I'm a woman. He hates women.

MAX   He doesn't hate women. He just hates her.

SOPH   No you should go. You're a man. He'll defer
to you. Go on, go and have a chat with Ali.

MAX   No way I'm going. He'll kill me.
I can't just drop in and pretend to be pally.
I know my facts.
More police are killed in America for intervening in DV
than in any other kind of criminal activity.

SOPH   You're not the police and this isn't America, Max.

MAX   I don't think it's the uniform that provokes them.

SOPH   We have to stop it. I can't stand it. I can't stand it
anymore.

MAX   We could phone the police.

SOPH   They'd know it was us.

MAX   No. It could be anyone within a local radius.
You do one of your impersonations
and we can remain anonymous.

SOPH   What would we say? If we can't *see* we can't prove it.

MAX   We don't have to prove it. We just have to stop it.

SOPH   We can't stop it if we don't prove it.

MAX   No. He just needs to know. If he knows that we know
he'll stop.

SOPH   He won't.

MAX   He will. He might.

SOPH   If he knows that we know he'll kill her.

MAX   If he knows that we know he'll kill us.

SOPH   I think we should move.

MAX   They should bloody move.

SOPH   Go to the countryside and grow our own potatoes.

MAX   Why? I don't want to go anywhere where everyone knows what everyone's doing and everyone thinks the same. I'd rather die.

SOPH   Sssh. It's gone quiet.

MAX   Oh no.

SOPH   What can you hear?

MAX   You can hear the clock tick.

Silence.

What I don't understand – I don't get why she puts up with him. She's a very attractive woman. It's not as if she wouldn't have the pick.

SOPH   You fancy her?

MAX   I've never been attracted to a white woman in my life. As you well know.

SOPH   She's not white, Max.

MAX   Well she's not *black* either. Maybe he's just good in the sack.

SOPH   I don't care if he's Casabloodynova. What he's doing to her now has nothing to do with love and I will not stand by while someone else is lying down and being fucked.

MAX   Over.

SOPH   OVER.

MAX   No, but we have to be careful.
        We're talking domestic violence.

SOPH   We live in a civilised world, Max,
        and it's the responsibility of people like you
        and people like me to stand up to people like him.
        You can't protest in silence.

        Silence.

MAX   If she was pregnant –

SOPH   She's not. She says she's not.

MAX   But if she was. We'd have to do something then.

SOPH   Because?

MAX   Because. If it involved another generation.
        Well, we'd act straight away then, wouldn't we?

SOPH   Of course we would.

MAX   No question.

SOPH   Of course.

MAX   Without hesitation.

        *BOBBY hits his target; a bird drops out of the sky. He
        examines it, then shoots it again at close range. And again.
        And again.*

        *ALI walks into the garden with a watering can. He waters
        his plants meticulously.*

ALI   You got there?

BOBBY   I heard.

ALI   You what?

BOBBY   Dead bird.

ALI   Good shot.

Silence.

BOBBY   She comin out?

ALI   I dunno. Jesus. You trying to make me lose count?

BOBBY   How long they gonna take?

ALI   They're already comin up, look, you can see the little
shoots.

BOBBY   What about the weather?

ALI   What about the weather?

BOBBY   Why don't you plant it there where it's sunny?

ALI   Far too dry, innit. They'd get the full brunt.

BOBBY   I'd like to be a gardener.

ALI   Don't be a cunt.
You need to get a proper job,
earn a bit of money.

BOBBY   I'm still at school, Dad.

ALI   You can't go on hanging about for ever,
drivin us all mad.
She'll have the kid soon
you'll have to get yourself together.

BOBBY   But I live here.

ALI   What's the matter with you anyway?
You got to leave home some time.
You gay?

BOBBY   Fuck off.

ALI   Hey.

BOBBY   I just like the idea of plants and that.
         You show me how to do it?

ALI   You takin the piss?

BOBBY   No!

ALI   Come here you stupid prat.
         Hold this.

Scene 5

MAX is constructing an eco-loo. SOPH is reading from the newspaper.

HANA is cleaning. She is heavily pregnant. She follows the conversation between MAX and SOPH intently, but dusts vigorously to disguise her interest. MAX and SOPH barely notice her.

MAX   'Connect plates while extending the base.'
         I hate it when they do this.
         What do they think I am?
         A contortionist?
         It's nothing like the diagram.
         Look. Completely different shape.

SOPH   You're going to have to explain to me just how
         exactly how a prostitute can claim rape.

MAX   And what's this supposed to connect with now?
         Useless piece of flex.

SOPH   I mean that's what she's there for.
        So it can hardly come as a surprise, can it? Sex.

MAX   Doesn't even fit.

SOPH   Max?

MAX   What?

SOPH   How can there be any question of force?
        What else has he come for but intercourse?

MAX   Who are we talking about?

SOPH   Doesn't matter who. She's a prostitute claims she's been
        raped. That's all you need to know.

MAX   Where?

SOPH   In the paper. Here.

MAX   No, *where*?

SOPH   Does it matter? Walthamstow. That's not the point. Who
        cares? / I'm saying how can you accuse someone of

MAX   I mean where did this happen? In the bedroom?
        Bathroom? Halfway up the stairs?

SOPH   violating someone else – in the bedroom, alright, in the
        bedroom, I

MAX   Alright, okay, the bedroom. Fine. (*He discovers some
        components he thought missing.*) At last. The screws.

SOPH   *said* if the person they're accused of raping
        is just lying there waiting?
        By accepting payment she's giving her consent.
        It's like a bank clerk accusing a customer of theft.

MAX   Well if he was wearing a balaclava and pointing a gun it
would be.

SOPH   What?

MAX   If he stole the money and left.

SOPH   No. Hold on. Hold on.
You go to a prostitute, that's what you pay for,
So it can't be stolen.

MAX   *Who.*

SOPH   What?

MAX   *Who* you've paid for, not what.

SOPH   Look. Listen, Max.

MAX   Maybe he didn't pay. The rapist. Maybe he just didn't
pay.

SOPH   Don't be funny.
That makes him a thief. Not a rapist.
It's nothing to do with money.

MAX   No, theft is if he stole her necklace while they're having
sex.
It relates to objects.
The definition of theft
/ is an appropriation of property belonging to somebody

SOPH   I know what theft is, Max. Please.
Don't start speaking legalese.

MAX   with the intention of permanently depriving them of it.
Okay, what I'm saying
is maybe he had sex and then tried to escape without
paying.

SOPH   No, that can't be right.

MAX   No, okay, it can't. There'd have to be some sort of
        struggle.

SOPH   Exactly.

MAX   You can't claim rape in hindsight.

        *Pause. HANA has been standing still for a while. Aware of
        the silence, she suddenly starts dusting vigorously again.*

        Maybe he changed his mind.

SOPH   What?

MAX   Let's say they agreed on a blow job
        right, so out comes the old knob
        suddenly he decides he'd rather take her from behind
        she says no, runs to the window
        shouts for help from a passing taxi
        – too late, he throws her down and takes her up the
        jacksie.

SOPH   Well that would be

MAX   A shock.

SOPH   Yes.

MAX   It would be

SOPH   Awful.

MAX   If it's not what they agreed. Yes.

SOPH   It would be –

MAX   A violation. Of their agreement.

SOPH   Yes but does that make it unlawful?

        *HANA knocks over her can of woodspray. Picks it up, drops
        it again, picks it up, drops it again. Recovers.*

Let's say he's into S and M, alright –

MAX   Who?

SOPH   it's her job – the client –
to pretend
but what's to stop him really being violent?
How can she claim it's against her will
if her will is something she has to suspend?

MAX   No, no, that can't be right.
By that definition she's raped six times a night.

SOPH   But violence is part of the business of whoredom.
/ Goes with the territory, doesn't it.

MAX   Not necessarily, no.

SOPH   It is, it's part of the job, it must be
– like being shouted at if you're a traffic warden.

MAX   I don't think we
should assume that what goes on inside the room
is kinky.
Mostly it's just sex
without the burden of any emotional context.

SOPH   Burden?

MAX   Yes. She's just fulfilling a function.

SOPH   Okay, then if her role is just to provide a hole
for him to hide in
then he can do whatever he likes to her without
compunction.

HANA lets out a low moan.

MAX   No.

SOPH   Yes.
        If she's just lying there, whatever,
        no one's trying to force her
        (Except of course society
        but that's something else altogether).

MAX   If you weren't a woman I'd say you were a misogynist.
        Why are you so hard on her and not so hard on the
        man?

SOPH   Men can't help being dickheads; women can.

        HANA stands to speak. But nothing comes out.

MAX   Sorry?

HANA   I go upstair.

MAX   Sorry?

HANA   I go.

MAX   Where?

HANA   Upstair.

MAX   Oh.

        *HANA grabs a bottle of detergent and a cloth and rushes
        upstairs.*

SOPH   God, I forgot she was there.

MAX   Hardly surprising, she's mute.

SOPH   What if she thinks we're talking about her?

MAX   We're not.

SOPH   But what if she thinks we are?

MAX   Soph. She's not a prostitute.

SOPH   No but I mean, no, I mean –
        you don't think she – you don't think he –
        do you think she's alright?

MAX   What? Why?

SOPH   Haven't you noticed? She's got a black eye.

MAX   No she hasn't.

SOPH   She has. It's huge. Can't you tell?
        Well, she is pregnant I suppose, isn't she?

MAX   Generally speaking, black eyes
        are not a symptom of pregnancy.

        MAX holds out the half-built eco-loo.

        Look, now it's coming along quite well.

        HANA comes charging downstairs.

HANA   What's happ to the toilet?

SOPH   Sorry?

HANA   Is gone.

SOPH   Oh yes, sorry, I forgot to say.

HANA   They's a big hole in the floor.

SOPH   We're making a new one. Look. Don't worry.

MAX   That's we as in me as in I am.

SOPH   It's dry. It's made from an easy kit.

MAX   Easy for you to say.

SOPH   You're the one said it's a no-brainer.

HANA   You sit on this?

MAX   Nononono, that's just the container.

SOPH   What you do –
        it doesn't use any water, you see
        it's an eco-loo
        it works on this batch system, so to speak.
        You rotate your four containers
        and replace them when they're full.
        It saves two hundred litres a week
        and there's no waste at all.

MAX   Apart from yours, of course.

SOPH   Yes, but even that's not lost
        you spread it round the garden and use it for your
            compost.

HANA   Compost.

SOPH   Yes, compost, you know.

HANA   You mean – you mean –

SOPH   That stuff you put it in the garden to make things grow.

HANA   You put your your your

SOPH   Waste.

HANA   Shit.

SOPH   Yes, alright, in the garden, yes.

MAX   But not straight away. It would stink.

SOPH   No, you can use it after six months, I think.

HANA   In the garden.

SOPH   It's alright. There's nothing in it now.

HANA   I'm not touching it.

HANA retches.

SOPH   Oh God, are you alright?

HANA   I'm sick.

SOPH   The baby.

HANA   No.

SOPH   Why don't you sit down and have some tea?

HANA   No thank you no.

SOPH   Is there something you want to tell us, Hana?

HANA shakes her head.

I don't mean just about this, now.
It's just – your – you – your face – somehow –
you look – doesn't she, Max?

MAX   Why don't you sit down Hana?

SOPH   You're not your usual self today.

Pause.

HANA   Your own waste.

SOPH   Look forget about the toilet, right.
Is there something you want to say?

HANA   No.

SOPH   You can trust us, you know.

HANA   For what?

SOPH   You should get angry sometimes Hana.

HANA   I do.

SOPH   You don't. You've got a very *placid* manner / which is

HANA   I do.

SOPH   good but now and then we all need to shout –
        no, you should.

HANA   I do.

SOPH   You don't though do you.

HANA   Monday I did.
        I'm standing in a bus queue,
        the driver, he starts makin a fuss
        cos none of us got no ticket
        account of the ticket machine is bust.
        He says to us – he says to go and get them from the
          shop
        but when we come back out again he starts drivin off
        an now what was a big queue has gotten even bigger –
        but he won't let us on, will he, stupid ugly nigger.
        So I get right in front the bus and then I start to cuss
        – jus like you tell me –
        I say to him I say I hope you get cancer and your kids
          are H I V.

        Silence.

MAX   Well it's a point of view.

SOPH   So. Was that a yes for tea?

HANA   I can't tho, I'm on duty.

        Pause.

SOPH   I know I know I know!

MAX   What?

SOPH   How a prostitute can be raped.

MAX   How?

SOPH   When she's off duty.

MAX   Right.

SOPH   When she's not being a prostitute. You see?

MAX   Of course.

SOPH   Makes sense.
         When she's a normal woman.
         Then it would be an offence.

Scene 6

*The sound of a baby crying. BOBBY comes running out into
the garden. Fumbles in his pocket, brings out a matchbox.
He lights a match and, watching it burn, begins to quieten
down. Does it again. Until he's calm.*

Scene 7

ALI and HANA's.

*The sound of the crying baby is coming from a tape recorder
which HANA cradles in a baby carrier. SOPH, MAX and ALI
are all standing around, coo-ing over it.*

MAX   She sleeping alright?

SOPH   She's beautiful.

HANA   Thank you.

MAX   I mean at night.

ALI   Sometimes. She sleeps, yeah. Sometimes she, you know, she just

MAX   Feeds.

ALI   Feeds, yeah. Depends on her, whatever,

MAX   Needs.

ALI   Yeah, she's a good girl, in't ya? In't ya princess girlie?

SOPH   She's so small. Size of her feet.

HANA   She come early.

SOPH   How much?

HANA   Six weeks.

SOPH   Wow.

HANA   She come in under. But she's doin alright now.

SOPH   Look at her wiggle her fingers. Sweet.

MAX   I'm not even going to say who she looks like.

ALI   What?

MAX   Oh come on. Look at the chin.

ALI   What's wrong with it?

MAX   Nothing. But look. No question who's the dad.

ALI   Who?

MAX   Come off it mate, she's you.

ALI   No she in't. She don't look nothing like me, she's a girl innit.

MAX   She does, look, she does, she's the bloody spit.
         You should be glad.

ALI   Hey.

MAX   What?

ALI   In front of the ladies.

MAX   I'm telling you, mate, she's you in drag
         isn't she, Soph?

SOPH   Yes, she is similar, yes.

ALI   No, she looks like her jaddah.
         Don't ya, my princess.

SOPH   We brought this. It's just, you know, a little thing. Hope
         she likes it.

         SOPH hands HANA a soft toy, unwrapped.

HANA   Oh thank you.

ALI   Nice one.

HANA   Very kind.

ALI   Yeah, cheers.

HANA   What is it?

SOPH   It's a mouse.

ALI   Course. Big ears.

HANA   A mouse. Look.

MAX   She smiled. Look. She's smiling at me.

ALI   She likes her mouse innit, ey, you never seen one of
         those.

MAX   She did it again. There. Look. Is she smiling at you or
      me?

HANA   I don't know, her eyes sometime go cross.

ALI   Stop flirting with the boss.
      He's too old for you, inne?

SOPH   Don't worry. She's got her eyes closed.
      I was torn
      between that and a pink chicken
      but you know they're colourblind,
      babies, when they're born?
      So in the end I bought a grey one.
      The woman in the shop said it's all the same to them,
      colour or no colour
      not because it was cheaper. I mean it wasn't cheaper,
      it was – well, it wasn't.

ALI   Sweet little mousey, in't she, ey?

SOPH   I know, I was almost tempted to keep her.

      The baby starts up again.

ALI   What's a matter now?

SOPH   Probably us. We should let you get on.

ALI   You fed her?

HANA   I just fed her.

ALI   So what's wrong?

SOPH   Max.

MAX   Yes, we should go.

ALI   No it's not you.

SOPH   She tired?

ALI   How much d'you feed her?

HANA   I don't know.

ALI   You didn't feed her enough, she's still hungry, look at her.

HANA   I don't know.

ALI   Go and feed her.

HANA   I just did.

ALI   You gotta feed her again.

HANA   Don't think there's nothing left.

ALI   How'd you know?

HANA   I can tell.

ALI   You don't know.

HANA   I can feel it.

ALI   You can't feel it. How can you feel it then?

HANA   It's probably wind innit.

ALI   She's the one crying.
        (*Indicating HANA to MAX.*) She can't feel it. How can she feel it?

        BOBBY enters.

MAX   Alright Bobby.

SOPH   Hi.

        He acknowledges them with a nod, settles in a corner and fiddles with his phone.

I think you look really well, Hana.
Don't you think? Considering.
Good colour in your cheeks.

ALI   It's gonna be six weeks.

SOPH   What?

ALI   When she gets her figure back.
It's all the all the milk, type thing.

The baby's still crying. ALI scrapes the chair back and stands abruptly. He glares at HANA.

Give it here. come on.

HANA reels back as though struck. Recovers, and faces him.

HANA   She's just settling.

ALI   No she's not. She's making a din.

The baby begins to quieten down.

Put her down then. She wants to sleep, put her down.

HANA   She's tired.

ALI   She's tired you gotta put her down
or she'll wake up with you jiggin around.
Put her down.

The baby stops crying. HANA goes to lay her down. She starts up again.

Too late. Give it here. (*To MAX and SOPHIE.*) She don't know. (*To HANA.*) Come here.

He grabs the baby off HANA.

It's her first and all that
but my mum's coming over any day.

> She'll sort it out.
> You've got to guess what they're tryin
> to say, what're they after, why are they crying
> how to please em, when to pick em up
> when to tease em, when to shut em up
> – see, she has, she's shuttup now, no reason.
> That's girls for you, innit.

MAX   They say the more noise the better.
         Reminds them of the womb.

ALI   We got enough, this room.
       There you go. Now she's happy.

SOPH   Maybe she needed a change.

ALI   What?

SOPH   A new nappy.
        Did you know – there's this van
        that will come and take your nappies away?
        What you do – you hand them over, dirty, to the man
        – not every day, once a week

ALI   Oh man.

SOPH   and they return them good as new.

MAX   So what's the drawback?

SOPH   It's quite expensive, I'm afraid
        but it's worth it ecologically –
        you know how long it takes a nappy to degrade?
        Two million years and that's a conservative estimate.
        But think – how many nappies does a baby use?
        Say five in the day and maybe three, at first, at night.
        Three years of nappies, well at that rate, what?
        Max? Let's just say a lot.
        I could get the number for you if you like.

ALI goes to put the baby down. She starts crying.

ALI   You take it. Here.

He hands her back to HANA and walks away. She quietens down in HANA's arms.

You want some coke, man?

MAX   What?

ALI   Or a beer?

MAX   Oh *coke*, no thanks, no.

ALI   You want one?

SOPH   No, thanks, nothing, I'm fine.

MAX   We should go. We really just came round to say hello.

SOPH   Yes, look at us.
As if you didn't have enough
To do. Have you had a lot of visitors?

ALI   Police came yesterday.

SOPH   Oh.

ALI   Yeah, someone called the cops.

SOPH   Why would they do that?

ALI   Because we're not English.

HANA   Ali.

ALI   Noise, they said.

MAX   What kind of noise?

ALI   They said we was noisy.

SOPH   In what way?

HANA   The baby.

ALI   Yeah, the baby.

BOBBY gets up and gets himself a coke.

SOPH   Oh but that's terrible. Babies cry all the time.
       You don't call the police.

MAX   That's what they do. You have babies, you don't expect
          peace.

SOPH   Who was it?

ALI   They should have come over and said something
       instead a goin to the fuzz
       but they don't talk to us,
       do they, them Greeks?
       With their fur and their bling
       and their minging statues out the front with stupid puffy
          cheeks.

HANA   It wasn't them what called the police.

ALI   Who was it then? She don't know.
       I tell you what I'm gonna do.
       Next time he parks his piece of tin in front of me
       I might have to take it for a spin
       and wrap it round a tree.

MAX   I wouldn't do that, Ali

ALI   You wouldn't have to.

SOPH   So who who do you think it was then, Hana?

HANA   Dunno, but it wan't them.
       She give me a baby clothes parcel.

ALI   If it wan't them I dunno –
        some other nosey arsehole
        (pardon me, / I'm sorry. Pardon me.)

SOPH   What? Oh, honestly Ali, don't mind me.

        HANA puts the baby down. It yells.

ALI   You do that for?

HANA   My arm.

MAX   Come on. / It's us. We should leave you alone.

ALI   What?

HANA   It hurt.

ALI   You didn't have to put her down.

SOPH   And thanks for the thanks for the –

MAX   Having us over.

SOPH   Thank you for having us round and all that.

ALI   Yeah, it's nice you come. Cheers.
        And thanks for the rat.

MAX   Oh my god, it's one o' clock.

SOPH   Is it?

ALI   Cheers for comin' over, yeah?

MAX   No, it's good to have something to celebrate.

SOPH   Come on Max or we're gonna be late.

        They go.

        Silence. ALI glares at HANA.

        BOBBY goes over to the baby. Stands there, staring at it.

HANA   What?

ALI   What?

HANA   What is it?

ALI   You could of given her me. You never –

HANA   What?

ALI   Why'd you put her down?

HANA   I can't hold her forever, Ali.

ALI   Why didn't you give her me?

HANA   She would have woke anyway.

ALI   You shouldn't of put her down.

HANA   Ali.

ALI   Tryin to be clever.
       What dyou think I am? a fucking clown?

       BOBBY makes to pick up the baby.

       (*Without turning round.*) Don't pick it up.

Scene 8

MAX and SOPH.

SOPH   Shall we get these solar panels then?

MAX   What happens if we imagined it?

SOPH   We did not imagine anything.
        You saw the way he spoke to Hana.
        They're not what you'd think, they're much less.

MAX   But we haven't actually – we're speculating –
        we haven't actually seen him hit
        her. What if he denies it?

SOPH   He will deny it. Of course he will.
        He's not going to just confess.
        You just have to go in and confront him.

MAX   Then what?

SOPH   You hit him. Guess how much. Go on, guess.

MAX   I need to get him to trust me.

SOPH   Nine hundred all in.

MAX   Soph?

SOPH   Shall we?

MAX   NO.

SOPH   Okay.

MAX   I need a pretext. I can't just go in bald.

SOPH   Just go and ask for sugar. I told you.

MAX   We have to make it easy for him to talk.

SOPH   No, we have to make it impossible for him not to.

MAX   I don't want him to think that I judge him.

SOPH   Why not? You do.

MAX   We have to try and see things from his point of view.

SOPH   Oh don't be such a liberal woolly,
        you don't try and *understand* a bully.

MAX   You can, you should, you have to
        find out what drives him to it.

SOPH   She does. Obviously.

MAX   Yes, but *how*?

SOPH   No, I mean, no, I mean, *Max*. / I was being facetious

MAX   Do you think it's because –

SOPH   What?

MAX   I don't mean because they're Turkish –

SOPH   They're not.

MAX   I don't mean to sound –
        you know – but it could be to do with their culture
        or something in his background
        it'll be down to some trauma or other
        usually it's the mother.

SOPH   Jesus.

MAX   No, you have to look at the whole
        person, cos most of the time he's quite a nice bloke.
        He must just lose control
        sometimes. Maybe it's the coke.

SOPH   So how come he hasn't killed her yet?
        He's twice her size, don't forget.
        He must be fourteen stone and she'll be nine at most
        if he really lost control then she'd be dead.
        But no self-respecting parasite is going to kill off its host.

MAX   You know what I mean.

SOPH   No. I don't.

MAX   I don't think he contrives
        to lose his temper's what I'm saying.
        Now and again we all do
        but most of us don't go hitting our wives

(however much we'd like to) –
he obviously can't help it.

SOPH   You make it sound as if it's fate.
It's not. It's controlled. And it's hate.
The question you should ask
is if he lost his temper down the pub would he hit his
    mate?

MAX   Not necessarily –

SOPH   No. He wouldn't hit a man.
It's nothing to do with losing control.
He hits her because she's a woman. He hits her because
    he can.

MAX   That doesn't make sense.

SOPH   No it doesn't make sense.
Don't laugh.
It doesn't make sense that women make up more than
    half the population and earn less than two percent of
    its wealth.

MAX   What?

SOPH   It doesn't make sense that I'm married to you.
It's a well known fact that marriage is bad for your
    health
and women who don't marry live longer than women
    who do
but here I am, for some reason, in that ridiculous role –
not for much longer though
if you're going to take the side of an arsehole.

MAX   Look, all I'm saying is
maybe she colludes, is all I'm saying.
We don't know half their business

but she must have her reasons for staying.
If she really couldn't take it, she'd go.

SOPH   If he found out she was leaving she'd be lucky to get out
            alive
        and he'll have made sure she's dependent on him to
            survive.

MAX   But you have to admit though.

SOPH   What?

MAX   You have to admit.

SOPH   WHAT?

MAX   Don't shout. I'm just saying she can be capricious.

SOPH   Does that mean she deserves to be knocked about?

MAX   Of course it doesn't. But one minute
        she's mute and meek and mild
        the next she's like Alf bloody Garnett.

SOPH   So maybe she is, maybe she can be annoying
        maybe she's always late, maybe she burns his dinner
        maybe she drinks, maybe she stinks
        maybe she used to be thinner
        and now he just finds her cloying
        or maybe she really did something heinous,
        had an affair, laughed at his penis
        – no, let me speak, okay –
        let's say she makes him feel small, weak,
        she makes him think of his mum,
        she reminds him of the boy he was
        and the bastard he's become.
        There'll be something to do with his parents or sex
        some unresolved Oedipus complex
        or maybe he'd rather sleep with his father,

alright, okay, so there's bound to be a reason he's a shit
and she probably represents it
so when she appears and holds out her hand
for affection, a fiver, a lift, whatever
– *something he can't give* –
does that give him permission
to batter her into submission
or beat her to death?
She still has the right to live.

MAX   Okay. Forget it.

SOPH   What?

MAX   Save your breath.
If there's only one side to the story
and we don't even want to hear what it is
how can I ask him to listen to me?
He'll say it's none of my business.
You have to think of how he'll react
given what his offence is.
If we go in without a plan
there will be consequences.
No, you're right. I think we should avoid all conflict if
  we can.

Pause.

SOPH   Right.

MAX   Okay?

SOPH   Fine.

MAX   Good. So. Where would these solar panels go?

SOPH   Fuck the solar panels.

MAX   No. Really, I want to know.

SOPH   I don't give a shit.
             You could stick them up your arse if I thought they'd fit.

MAX   Tell me.

SOPH   No.

MAX   It's a good idea. I agree we should put some up. Where?

SOPH   I told you, you've just forgotten because you don't care.

MAX   I do or I do or I wouldn't be asking.

SOPH   You read the statistics same as me.
             We're going to run out of fuel by 2023 –
             these aren't just my neurotic fears –
             the increase in climate change was more last century
             than in the last ten thousand years
             but you're clearly far too busy
             to notice that the world's about to end,
             so why don't you just fuck off with your new wife-
               beating friend.

MAX   Sophie. Stop it. It's not my fault.

SOPH   DON'T TOUCH ME OR I'LL DO YOU FOR
             ASSAULT.

             Silence. *

MAX   If you're a hundred percent sure, then –

SOPH   I don't have any doubt.

MAX   No. Nor do I.

SOPH   It's illegal now as well you know, not to put your bins
             out.

MAX   So what do you want to do?

SOPH   Not up to me, is it? You're the *man.* It's up to you.

Scene 9

HANA, comes on and starts here * almost to herself, and
then repeats and continues, to us.

HANA   If I were a house
I'd be fallen down
windows all broke
holes in the floor
roof half off
so much dust it make you choke
no front door.

I need a place to hide
and I seen one just like it
near where I catch the number twenty-three
so I go inside
reminds me of me
place is fulla rotten wood
and rubbish
bugs crawling everywhere
smells bad, like fish;
don't bother me
it feels good.

There int no proper walls
ceiling's low
and full of holes
must be a bed up there cos I can see a pillow,
but you can't get up there
cos they's only half a stair.

Then I see a mouse
and I don't like mice
I says come here mousey
(I'm good at that
pretending to be nice)

but he run off
– he might of bin a rat –
jus as well he did
if he'd a come nearer
I'd of squashed the bastard flat.

Don't want no one in my home
not even a mouse
like I said
just want to be left alone
with stuff what's empty, broken, dead;
it's me it is, this house.

I like the dirt
I like the dark
if no one can see me I in't nobody's wife
and I forget to hurt
I like to hear nothing but the sound of my own breath
I like to hide
I don't believe in life
but I know there's somethin after death
cos I already died.

Scene 10

ALI's. MAX and ALI.

MAX   I'm telling you – / I'm asking you – no, listen

ALI   What I do in my private – it's got nothing to do with
      you.
    What's it got to do with you?

MAX   – I'm saying you can't, Ali, you cannot – it has
      everything to do with me. I am your neighbour. / I saw
      you. Standing on the doorstep in front of

ALI   What I do – it's none of your – fuck off. I int never done
      nothing – what doorstep? I int never done nothin

MAX   the whole – you did, yes, doorstep, your doorstep.

ALI   on my doorstep. Why would I do it on my doorstep?

MAX   well I don't know but I saw you on the doorstep – / how

ALI   Bollocks.

MAX   else would I – how else would I know?

ALI   Who told you?

MAX   Nothing. No one. I said. I saw you / right in front – are

ALI   You can't of.

MAX   you denying it?

ALI   I int never done nothing on no doorstep.

MAX   You are a lying git.
      I bloody saw you.

ALI   Who told you?

MAX   Right, so you admit it.

ALI   Who told you this?

MAX   No one told me, alright?
      I saw you with my own eyes in broad bloody daylight.

ALI   Someone told you.

MAX   No one told me.

ALI   Someone must've said something.

MAX   I'm telling you, Ali – are you listening? / I know

ALI   It was her, wan't it? She told you.

MAX   because I – no one fucking told me. I saw.

ALI   What she wanna do that for?

MAX   Look. Listen. It's got nothing to do with Hana, alright.
I didn't need to be told.

ALI   So why bring her into it?

MAX   I didn't. You did.

ALI   She fucking told you.

MAX   Jesus / it's like arguing with a two-year-old.

ALI   What did she say then? What did she say?

MAX   NOTHING. At all.

ALI   You know what, Max. I like you and that,
but what I do in my own house is none of your fucking
business, mate.

MAX   It is exactly my business.

ALI   I don't even want to have this debate.

MAX   I am a witness – I've actually seen you at it –
so it's very much my business.

ALI   Yeah? Well whatever you saw, you think you saw,
it's got fuck all to do with you.

MAX   It has everything to do with me –
I'm your *neighbour* unfortunately
so I cannot ignore –
I will not stand by –
if I see someone doing something I deplore –

ALI   Fucking – what's your problem, man?
        It's my business what I do on my own fucking patch.

MAX   Patch?

ALI   Patch, house, whatever, *home*. What's the big deal?

MAX   It's not just *your* business,
        my friend – try saying that to the law
        they might just think you're taking the piss.

ALI   You gonna squeal?

MAX   It is *illegal.*

ALI   Go on then. Call the fucking fuzz.

MAX   It is, you know, it is a criminal offence.

ALI   You think they're interested in me? You think they give
        a fuck about my little criminal fence?

MAX   I didn't say I'm going to call them, / I just told you it's
        not legal.

ALI   Go ahead. Call the cops. Go on. Here's my phone.
        You think you got evidence –

MAX   Look – this isn't about the fucking police
        alright? I just came round to talk. To reason.
        In the name of peace.

ALI   That's nice, innit. How polite.

MAX   I'm not interested in the law. I'm a barrister.
        That's not what this is about. I'm interested in stopping
        you before they find out.

ALI   I'm careful.

MAX   No. Careful isn't good enough.
       The law is not equivocal when it comes to this sort of
          stuff.

ALI   But it's not like a frigging drugs ring.
       It's not my total income, is it?
       It's more a supplement, type thing.

MAX   It is illegal to sell drugs. Full stop.

ALI   Piss in the ocean, mate. Not even a drop.

MAX   How much?

ALI   What?

MAX   How much are you making? From my weed. How
          much?

ALI   You want a cut?

MAX   No I do not want a cut. I wouldn't touch
       it with a barge pole. I want to know how much
       you make and who are they – the people who buy it?

ALI   We got a customer base 'bout twenty-five.

MAX   Fuck's sake.

ALI   Thirty tops.

MAX   And who are these – *customer base* – who are these
          people?

ALI   You want their names?

MAX   No I don't want their fucking names you stupid sod.
       I want to know – where do they come from?
       How do you know them? How do you know – they're
          not part of some drug squad?

ALI   What, all of them?

MAX   How do you know you can trust them?

ALI   I don't trust them. Why should I trust them? I don't
         know them.

MAX   Exactly.

ALI   They just pay me. Cash.
         I don't care who they are
         long as they keep coming back
         for their hash.

MAX   You should care.

ALI   Don't worry about it, man.
         Give yourself a heartattack.

MAX   I am fucking worried about it.

ALI   Well don't fucking worry about it. / I'm not worried
         about it.

MAX   I am worried about it because, look, okay, listen. I am a
         barrister. / And as a barrister – SHUTTUP – as a

ALI   It's only – who cares what I –

MAX   member of the legal profession, I have to be above
         reproof.
         I can't be mixed up with this kind of *trade*.
         Now. I haven't done anything wrong
         but if a connection can be made –

ALI   You're the supplier innit?

MAX   If a connection can be made between you as the pusher
         and me as the person you got them from –

ALI   You gave me the seeds.

MAX   Thank you, yes, wasn't that nice of me? *Gave.*
      But the law might not see it as generosity.
      The law looks for signs of reciprocity.
      Now, you might not care if you get done
      but carry on like this and we'll both be in prison
      so you've got to fucking stop it.
      I gave you that stuff to smoke for your pleasure
      not deal on my bloody doorstep for profit.

ALI   My bloody doorstep, not your bloody doorstep.

MAX   Because I am complicit, you see, in your crime,
      and if they ever found out – which they will do –
      because the way you carry on it's only a matter of
        time –
      I cannot overstate the scale of the disaster that would
        ensue.
      You have no idea –
      if they ever found out and traced it back to me
      it would be the complete and total fucking end of my
        whole entire career.

ALI   Well that's alright then innit, cos I'm not telling them.

MAX   Well that's nice of you, Ali, why don't you give yourself
        a prize?
      If you wave it about on the fucking doorstep they don't
        need telling, do they? They just need eyes.

ALI   I don't do it on the doorstep. I said.
      They come round the back. But even if I did and I mean
        if. Because I don't, alright, so *if* the fuzz
      walked past and happened to notice me
      I'd just invite them in for a spliff.
      It's only class C.

MAX   Look you stupid backward fucking third world cunt.
This is England. There are laws.
You cannot bribe the police force.
Christ, I should never have let you in.
I don't give my weed to everyone, you know,
I trusted you – we've had you round for tea and cake –
I've even been nice to your delinquent bloody son –
and what happens? I find you're on the make.
You've no respect for me or anybody else's way of life
– well, if that's the way you want to play it, fine.
We've always had our doubts
about you, but I gave you the benefit – you think
   because I'm nice I've got no spine?
Fuck you. I don't hit my wife.
You're the loser. You're the coward. You're the one on
   handouts.
I should have said it years ago. Fuck you.

Silence.

ALI   You call the cops on me I'll call the cops on you.

MAX   Don't be ridiculous. I don't hit my wife.

ALI   You grow marijuana.

MAX   I don't hit my wife.

ALI   Fuck you.

MAX   Fuck you.

ALI   Fuck you.

MAX   Fuck YOU.

ALI   FUCK YOU.

MAX   Fine. But remember. She didn't tell me anything, alright.
I saw you myself. So don't go making up lies.

ALI   What?

MAX   I saw you on the doorstep, with my own eyes.

ALI   Fuck you.

Scene 11

ALI confronts HANA. He pushes up his shirtsleeves with manic repetition.

HANA stands near her baby which, at the moment, is silent.

HANA   Please.

ALI   Not please.

HANA   Sorry.

ALI   Sorry?

HANA   Sorry, I'm sorry, I'm sorry.

ALI   Good. What for?

HANA   Everything.

ALI   Fuck off.

HANA   Sorry.

ALI   (*Gesticulates towards the hi-fi.*) Go on then.

HANA   No, Ali, please.

ALI   Not PLEASE.

HANA   Sorry.

ALI   Fucking turn it fucking on.

HANA   They know anyhows.

ALI   How do they know?

HANA   How?

ALI   Good question.

HANA   How they know?

ALI   You tell me, go on, you tell me.

HANA   I don't know.

ALI   Shuttup.

HANA   I don't

ALI   Shuttup.

HANA   Know.

ALI   You what?

HANA   I don't know.

ALI   Shuttup. Turn it on.

HANA   I don't know something.

ALI   Nothing. You don't know nothing.

HANA   No

ALI   Not something.

HANA   I don't know.

ALI   How long have you been living in this fucking country?
        You don't know nothing. Not something. Say I don't
        know nothing.

HANA   I don't know nothing.

ALI   Is that right?

HANA   I don't know.

ALI   Turn it on. Go on. Turn it on.

HANA turns the radio on. A burst of classical music.

Not that.

HANA laughs

The fuck. Turn it off.

HANA   No.

ALI   Fucking turn it off.

HANA shakes her head.

Fucking turn that fucking racket fucking off.

HANA   No.

ALI   I said

HANA   NO NO NO NO NO NO NO.

He 'hits' her. Repeatedly. He doesn't actually make contact; the violence is ritualised, so that the moment of striking and the reaction to being struck are distinct and separate.

The baby starts crying.

Eventually, BOBBY appears in the doorway.

BOBBY   What's happening?

ALI   Leave it.

BOBBY   What's happened?

ALI   Get up will you. Fuck off.

BOBBY   What?

ALI   Will you fuck off will you fuck off?

BOBBY   Get up, Hana.

ALI   FUCKING GET UP.

Finally, she does. She's in between the two men. She holds up her hand; ALI hits it; the baby starts crying; he hits it again, and again. She turns from ALI to BOBBY. He hits her. ALI hits BOBBY. Repeatedly. The baby's cry gets louder, until BOBBY grabs the 'baby' and throws it on the floor. The tape rewinds, the crying stops. Silence.

Scene 12

MAX and SOPH's.

HANA, bruised and disfigured. She has a broken arm.

The scene takes place in two time frames at once: MAX, attending to HANA (shown here on the right); MAX, relating the incident to SOPH (on the left).

MAX   Oh my god oh my god oh my
                         god.

HANA   He's gone.

MAX   It's my fault.

SOPH   No, Max, it isn't. No.

HANA   I said to him to go.

MAX You should have seen her,
   Soph. We're talking first
   degree assault.

SOPH You told him we knew.
   That's all you did. What else
   were we supposed to do?

HANA   I said to him to go away. Don't
         never come back, I said.

MAX   What has he done to you Hana?

SOPH I thought you were going to
   say something worse. For
   a minute I thought she was
   dead.

HANA   They is animal. I don't never want
         to see them animal again.

SOPH What happened then?

HANA   / They is gone, I'm glad. They is
         gone.

MAX He's gone, she kept saying,
   that's all.

SOPH Where?

MAX I don't know. Just away.
         Have you called the police?

SOPH Yes, what did they have to say?

HANA   I in't telling them.

MAX They didn't come.

SOPH   She didn't phone them, did
        she?

HANA   No. Not them. No.

MAX   She's scared of another attack.

SOPH   But that's exactly why she
        should.
        He might come back.

MAX   I know but she's in an
        impossible position.
                        What will you do if he does come
                        back, Hana?

HANA   I won't let them in.

MAX   One, he's got the key. Two, I don't
                        think he'll be asking permission.

SOPH   Where does she think he's
        gone?

HANA   I dunno. To hell.

MAX   She said she didn't know. She
        wasn't lying, I could tell.
        He won't come back – he
        wouldn't dare.

SOPH   But what if he does?

MAX   That's what I asked her but she
        just said

HANA   No one does from there.

SOPH   How can she be so sure?

MAX   I'll kill him if he does
         And then she started crying.

SOPH   She would do, she's in shock.
         Even if he's a monster, they say
            it's like somebody dying.

MAX   I thought, well,
            maybe I shouldn't be so hard.
         I mean what if he does comes
            back from hell
         they make up, and we have
            to pretend to be nice to the
            bastard?

HANA   Only way I want em back is dead.
                            I hate them both.

MAX   / Both?

SOPH   Both?

HANA   Yeah, it's Bobby as well innit.

MAX   She told me – she said –

HANA   I wish he in't never been born.

MAX   I know she doesn't like him
         but I thought, funny thing to
            say.

SOPH   Surely not because – she did
            say something to me once
            about him being gay?

MAX   What happened? Hana? He didn't
                               hit you too? Did he?

SOPH   My god. I never dreamed.

MAX   She opened her mouth but
           nothing came out.
           The thing is, Soph, the thing
             is this, would any of this
             have happened if we hadn't
             intervened?

SOPH   Oh Jesus Christ, no, it's too late
             for that polemic.
           I mean, yes of course it would
             – the son as well?! –
           it's obviously endemic.

MAX   Hana. You've got to look after
                                 yourself.
                               There must be something I can
                                 do to help.
                               If either of them come back it
                                 won't just be for fun.
                               Do you understand?

HANA   Yes.

MAX   Good. What can I do?

HANA   Have you got a gun?

MAX   No, I don't have a gun.
                               Look. Violence is a cycle and we
                                 have to try and make it stop.

SOPH   We?

MAX   Yes. Whether we like it or not,
             she's now our responsibility.

SOPH   Since when did you become a
             cop?

We have to call the police, Max.
It's not our word against his
anymore. She's walking proof.
No one's going to buy that old
one of walking into a door.

MAX   Nobody saw him do it though,
did they?

SOPH   Except her son, by the sound of
it.

MAX   And she doesn't want to
involve the law.

SOPH   Well, she may not want to
pursue it
but if they have enough
evidence
they're compelled to ignore her
and press charges
the same way they would for
any offence.

MAX   But what about protecting her?
That's what she really needs
them for.
And that's when I noticed the
baby wasn't crying.

HANA   Sleepin, innit.

SOPH   So?

MAX   And there was something
unnatural in the way she was
lying.

SOPH   Maybe it was asleep.

MAX   That's what she said, but even if
             it was, I've never seen a baby
             lie so still.

SOPH   What are you getting at, Max?
             Why would you want the
             baby to cry?

MAX   Crying is a sign of life.
                                       Is she ill?

HANA   No.

MAX   What's wrong?

HANA   Nothing.

MAX   She picked her up, but her
             hands were shaking,
             the baby slipped and she only
             just caught her.

SOPH   She has to get away from here.
             She may not want to look after
             herself, but she has to protect
             her daughter.

MAX   Hana.

HANA   What?

SOPH   We need to find her a safe house.
             Somewhere she can disappear.

MAX   Is there somewhere he won't find
                                 you?

HANA   I in't goin nowhere. I'm stay here.

MAX   I don't mean forever. There must
                                   be somebody nearby
                                   – a cousin, a sister, a friend?

SOPH   Because he will come back.
            It's not a question of whether,
               it's more a question of when
               and why.

HANA   I got a uncle in Vermont.

SOPH   I mean she obviously can't stay
               here.

MAX   You can stay with us if you want.

SOPH   What the hell did you say that
               for?

MAX   There's the little room at the
               end.

HANA   Thanks but I int movin.

MAX   We are her only friend.

SOPH   Don't be ridiculous.

MAX   A temporary place to live.

SOPH   She cannot possibly stay with us.

MAX   I didn't see any alternative.

SOPH   You have to do these things by
               the book.
            That's what they say.
            Apart from anything else, it's
               the first place he'd look.

MAX   Second.

                                Look, it's really not a problem.
                                You can move in straight away.

SOPH   And for another, you're a man.

HANA   No. No, I'm stay.

SOPH   Are you completely / mad?

MAX   No. She can't stay on her own.

                                Is your pride more important than
                                    your life?

HANA   Is okay.

MAX   I said if she's not going to come
            here then I'd go over there.

SOPH   You what?

HANA   No no no way, thank you, no.

SOPH   What on earth is he going to
            think
        if he returns
        and finds you in bed with his
            wife?

MAX   I don't care what he assumes
        – he'd be wrong –
        anyway we'd have separate
            rooms.

SOPH   You cannot take over his house, Max.

MAX   Look. It didn't happen to you.
        I'm the one who told him to
            stop hitting his wife.
        I feel – I feel responsible –

SOPH   We're not talking about your
            feelings. We're talking about
            her life.

MAX   What do you think I'm talking
            about? She needs protecting.
            Obviously.
            And I can give her that.
            And I want her to know, not all
            men are like that twat.
            Anyway she likes me.
                                    Please. Think about it Hana.

HANA shakes her head.

SOPH   Really Max? That's nice.
            How do you know?

MAX   I just do.

SOPH   What did she say?

*HANA goes to speak. But touches MAX on the sleeve instead,
before rushing out.*

MAX   She sort of smiled and then she went.

SOPH   Did she say she wanted you in her house?

MAX   Not in so many words
            but I'm sure that's what she meant.

SOPH   Jesus Christ Almighty.

MAX   No listen, Soph –

SOPH   No, be quiet, you listen to me –
            you can't just go striding in,
            playing the good Samaritan – *wait* –
            the damage is already done.

I'm telling you, Max, *it's too late*.
He's done it before and he'll do it again
but you have no right to take over his house – are you
    insane?
Soon as he's gone you move in / thinking

MAX   To protect her, to protect her it's for her own sake.

SOPH   oh what luck – no, he won't give a fuck
what you think you're there for,
he'll just think you're on the make.
Just think of his *shame*.
He finds you in his house with her all it will do is
    inflame
him. / It's crap on every level – no – but

MAX   I don't care I don't care –
don't you see – she can't be on her own.

SOPH   well you bloody should – the worst thing is she doesn't
    even want you there
(and even if she did I wouldn't let her)
this is all about you
wanting to feel better.

MAX   No it is not.

SOPH   Yes it is. The only thing you can guarantee
is a night or two of false security
because think of the future, Max, and a future of *fucking
    hell.*
I mean *Jesus fucking hell.*
He's a monster, yes, and he's broken the law, but that
    doesn't mean you can as well.
When he comes back and finds you there, he may think,
    hang on, that's not fair
and he might just conclude
– I don't blame him – it figures –

it's just an elaborate ploy
for getting into her knickers.

MAX   Sophie. That's enough.

SOPH   I always knew you fancied her. Your little bit of rough.

MAX   Shuttup, I said, shuttup.

SOPH   Now he's gone, you've seen her scars,
the whole thing's turned you on –

MAX hits SOPH round the head.

I don't believe you did that.

MAX   I don't believe you said that.

SOPH   Words are just words are just. That hurt.

MAX   I'm sorry but I never ever flirt.

Silence.

SOPH   Come here.

MAX   No.

SOPH   You scared of me?

MAX   I think I know what coming there entails.

SOPH   What?

MAX   If you can speak you don't need to hit me;
violence is what happens when language fails.

Scene 13

BOBBY, in the garden of his house. He produces a box of matches. Strikes one, sets a piece of material alight and throws it through the window into his house. He watches it burn while he slowly backs away.

SOPH, lying in bed, alone.

SOPH   Don't know about you, Max,
but I can't sleep.
I've been lying here since three,
wishing I was someone else; I keep
going over what happened,
wishing you hadn't hit me.
But I miss you.
I know you're only next door
but it feels like another country
or like you've just gone off to fight some stupid war.
I can't sleep for thinking.
I know there's no solution
but my brain just won't stop,
what with that and all the light pollution.
Just look at that glow.
There are something like eleven thousand stars up there,
not that you can see a single one though.
From what I understand
too much artificial light at night can affect your pineal
    gland
and block production of your sleep hormone
or give you cancer.
But why is the sky so red
tonight?
I wish I hadn't said those things to you
I wish you hadn't hit me
I wish I'd hit you instead.
What a mess we're making of the universe.

I know what I said was wrong
but what you did to me was worse.
I mean, Jesus, I mean – shit –
I'm not the kind of woman who expects to be hit
I know my worth and –
– we're not that sort of person –
I'm practically a feminist and you're liberal by birth.
Oh God, that light.
I can't stop yawning.
I know everything's worse at night
and it'll all be fine in the morning.
You'll come back and I will forgive you
and I hope in the meantime you're being a good
  policeman, Max,
but I also hope, for conscience' sake, you're sleeping
  badly too.
God, will you look at the time? Nearly seven.
No point in going to sleep anymore
but I'm far too tired to get up.
I want to go back to the minute before
our row, when God was still in his heaven.
Unlike now.
He could be looking straight at me
but for all that light spill up there you can't even see the
  plough.
I'll write to the council tomorrow
and tell them what to do –
about the measures you can take to prevent sky glow.
It's not even dark
now and I cannot sleep for trying.

*Through the crackling of the flames we can hear the baby
start to cry next door. Getting louder and more insistent.*

Oh no that's the worst thing
the sound of a fox's bark

– or is it a baby crying?
Why can't I just relax?
There's this crackling noise in my head
– or can you hear it too, Max?
It's time to go to work now but I'm staying here in bed.
Why is the sky so red, this morning?
Why is the sky so red?

THE END